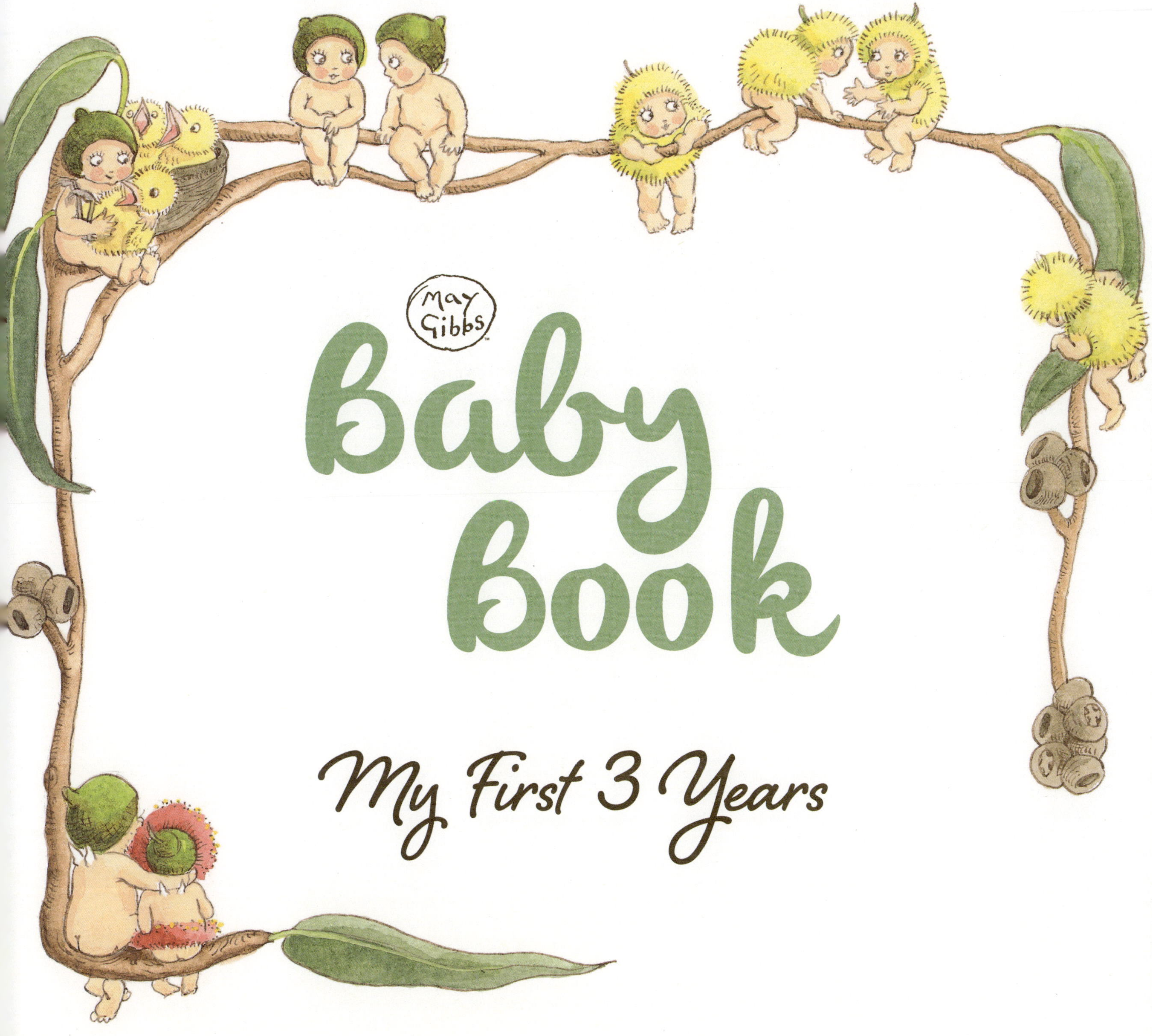

May Gibbs

Baby Book

My First 3 Years

A note for families:

This book is for mums and dads, and for caregivers and families of all kinds. Take your pen and make the book just right for your precious baby!

Illustrations created by Caroline Keys, inspired by May Gibbs' original works.

Published by Scholastic Australia in 2023.

Scholastic Australia Pty Limited
PO Box 579 Gosford NSW 2250
ABN 11 000 614 577
www.scholastic.com.au

Part of the Scholastic Group
Sydney • Auckland • New York • Toronto • London • Mexico City
New Delhi • Hong Kong • Buenos Aires • Puerto Rico

Designed by Cara Ord
Edited by Georgia Parry

ISBN 978-1-76129-945-2

Printed in China.

Scholastic Australia's policy, in association with its printers, is to use papers that are renewable and made efficiently from wood grown in responsibly managed forests, so as to minimise its environmental footprint.

My name is

____

All About my parents

Their name is ________________________________

They were __________ years old when I was born.

They are special because: ________________________

____

____

Photo of my parent

Photo of my parent

Their name is ______________________________

They were __________ years old when I was born.

They are special because: ______________________________

____

____

Other members of my family are ______________________________

____

Waiting for me to arrive

My parents first found out about me on ____________________

My due date was ____________________

This is how my parents told my family about me:

____

____

My parents first heard my heartbeat on ____________________

My parents first felt me kick on ____________________

OOF! I was strong!

My parents' hopes and dreams for my future:

____

____

____

____

____

____

Ultrasound photo

My scans showed:

- ☐ I was a boy
- ☐ I was a girl
- ☐ My parents wanted to be surprised

Here are a few names my parents thought of for me:

____

____

____

They decided to name me ____________________ because

____

____

My baby Shower

Shower invitation or photo

Guest and Gift list

Guest: ______________________ Gift: ______________________

Guest: ______________________ Gift: ______________________

Guest: ______________________ Gift: ______________________

Guest: ______________________ Gift: ______________________

Guest: ______________________ Gift: ______________________

Guest: ______________________ Gift: ______________________

Guest: ______________________ Gift: ______________________

Guest: ______________________ Gift: ______________________

Guest: ______________________ Gift: ______________________

Guest: ______________________ Gift: ______________________

Guest: ______________________ Gift: ______________________

Guest: ______________________ Gift: ______________________

Guest: ______________________ Gift: ______________________

Guest: ______________________ Gift: ______________________

Guest: ______________________ Gift: ______________________

Guest: ______________________ Gift: ______________________

Guest: ______________________ Gift: ______________________

My first Home

My first address was ______________________

____

____

Photo of our house

I love my room!

It was decorated ____________________

____

____

Photo of the nursery

I'm Here!

The first photo of me

I was born on ____________ at ________ AM / PM.

I was ☐ early ☐ on time ☐ late.

I weighed ____________ kilograms.

I was ____________ centimetres long.

I was born at ____________

My doctor was ____________

My eyes were ____________

My hair was ____________

Hospital bracelet

My birth story: ____________

What the World Was Like when I was born

The prime minister was ______________________________

Famous movies were ______________________________

Popular songs were ______________________________

A cup of coffee cost ______________ A litre of milk cost ______________

Here are some news headings from my first year

Little Me!

Here's my handprint

Here's my footprint

Look how tiny I am in this photo!

My Firsts

My first bath was on ______________

My first smile was on ______________

This is what made me smile: ____

____

My first laugh was on ______________

This is what made me laugh: ____

____

My first time sleeping through the night was on ______________

My first tooth came in on ______________

My first time eating solid foods was ______________

I ate ____

____

____

My first time crawling was on ____________________

My first word was ____________________

I said this on ____________________

My first steps were on ____________________

My first haircut was on ____________________

Photo of my first holiday celebration

The first holiday I celebrated was ____________________

My 1ST Month

I weighed ______________ kgs.

I was ______________ cm long.

Some things I liked to do: ______________________________

____

____

____

____

Some things I didn't like very much:

____

____

____

____

Photo at
1 month old

Photos

My 2ND Month

I weighed ______________________ kgs.

I was __________________________ cm long.

This made me smile: ____

____

____

____

____

This made me cry: _______________

____

____

____

____

Photo at
2 months old

Photos

My 3RD Month

I weighed ______________________ kgs.

I was ______________________ cm long.

Some things I discovered this month: ______________________________

____

____

____

Isn't that amazing?

Our favourite places to explore were:

____

____

____

Photo at
3 months old

Photos

My 4TH Month

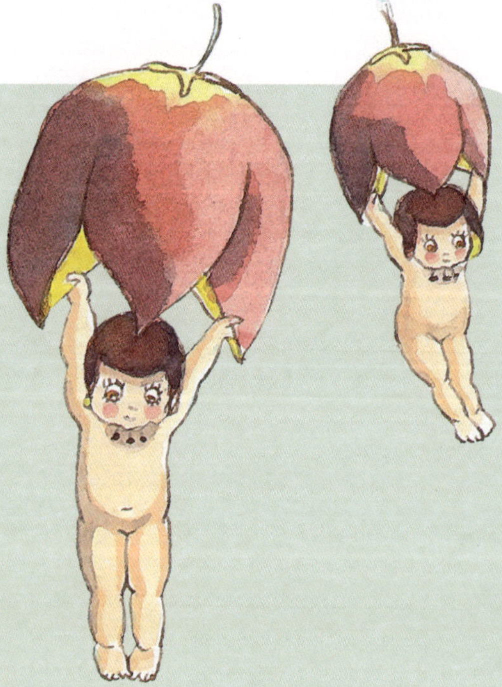

I weighed ______________________ kgs.

I was __________________________ cm long.

This made me happy: ____

____

____

This made me grouchy: __________

____

____

My favourite toys were: __________

____

____

____

Photo at
4 months old

Photos

My 5TH Month

I weighed ______________________ kgs.

I was ___________________________ cm long.

I was fascinated by: ____

____

____

____

Here's what I thought was scary:

____

____

____

____

____

Photo at
5 months old

Photos

My 6TH Month

I weighed ______________________ kgs.

I was __________________________ cm long.

My favourite food was: ____

____

____

Yum, yum!

But I did not like the taste of:

____

____

____

____

Photo at
6 months old

YUCK!

Photos

My 7TH Month

I weighed ______________________ kgs.

I was __________________________ cm long.

Things I learnt this month: ____

____

____

Some people I met: WOW!

____

____

____

____

(They thought I was adorable!)

Photo at
7 months old

Photos

My 8TH Month

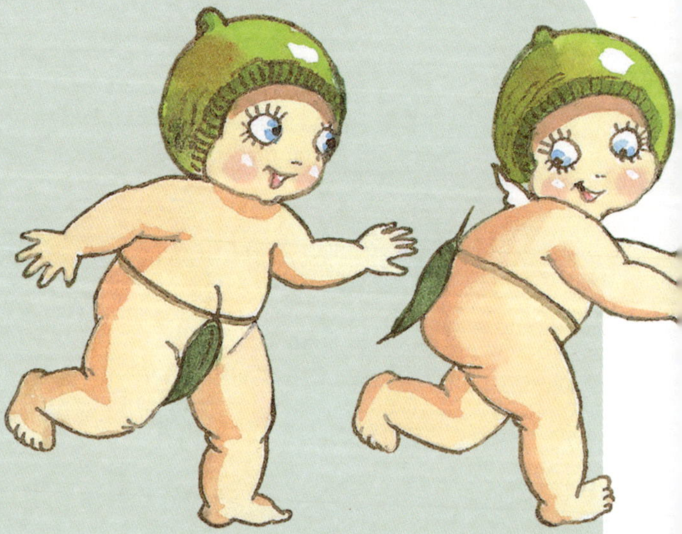

I weighed ______________________ kgs.

I was __________________________ cm long.

My favourite activity was: ____

____

____

____

My favourite books were: __________

____

____

____

____

____

Photo at
8 months old

Photos

My 9TH Month

I weighed ______________ kgs.

I was ______________ cm long.

I loved music, like ______________________________

When I heard it, I would ______________

Photo at 9 months old

Photos

My 10TH Month

I weighed ______________________ kgs.

I was __________________________ cm long.

Some words I could say were: ____

____

My friends were: ____

____

____

This is what we liked to play: _______

____

____

____

We had fun together!

Photo at
10 months old

Photos

My 11TH Month

I weighed ______________________ kgs.

I was ___________________________ cm long.

Can you believe how much I've grown?!

The world around me was so amazing. I was curious about ____________

____

____

____

____

I thought it was hilarious when _____

____

____

____

Photo at
11 months old

Photos

My 12TH Month

I weighed ______________________ kgs.

I was __________________________ cm long.

Some words I said were: ____

____

Here are some places I visited: ____

____

____

____

My favourite outing was: ___________

____

____

____

Photo at
12 months old

Photos

My first Birthday!

First birthday photo

Look how happy we were!

Here's what we did for my birthday: ______________________

____

Here's who was there: ______________________

____

My birthday cake was ______________________

Two years old!

Second birthday photo

Look how big I'm getting!

I weighed ____________________ kgs. I was ____________________ cm tall.

Here's what we did for my birthday: ____________________

____

My birthday cake was ____________________

At two, my favourite thing to do was: ____________________

Three
years old!

Third birthday photo

This was so much fun!

I weighed ______________ kgs. I was ______________ cm tall.

Here's how we celebrated my birthday: ______________

My birthday cake was ______________

My favourite things in the whole wide world were: ______________

____

How I Changed

Year One	Year Two	Year Three
Favourite food	Favourite food	Favourite food
Favourite toy	Favourite toy	Favourite toy
Favourite place	Favourite place	Favourite place
Favourite song	Favourite song	Favourite song
Favourite book	Favourite book	Favourite book

Getting Creative

Year One

My first scribble!

Wonderful Me!

Year Two

Here's a picture I drew of myself

And here is a photo of what I looked like

My Fantastic family

I am so lucky to be part of this family!
Here's a picture I drew of us

Year Three

And here is a photo of what we looked like